LIVES OF THE FEMALE POETS

Clare Pollard was born in Bolton in 1978 and lives in London. She has published six collections with Bloodaxe: *The Heavy-Petting Zoo* (1998), which she wrote while still at school; *Bedtime* (2002); *Look, Clare! Look!* (2005); *Changeling* (2011), a Poetry Book Society Recommendation; *Incarnation* (2017); and *Lives of the Female Poets* (2025). Her translation *Ovid's Heroines* was published by Bloodaxe in 2013. Her first play *The Weather* (Faber, 2004) premièred at the Royal Court Theatre. She works as an editor, broadcaster and teacher.

Her radio documentary, *My Male Muse* (2007), was a Radio 4 Pick of the Year. She co-edited the anthology *Voice Recognition: 21 poets for the 21st century* (Bloodaxe Books, 2009) with James Byrne, and translated Asha Lul Mohamud Yusuf's *The Sea-Migrations* (Somali title: *Tahriib*) with Maxamed Xasan 'Alto' and Said Jama Hussein (Bloodaxe Books/ The Poetry Translation Centre, 2017). Her non-fiction book *Fierce Bad Rabbits: The Tales Behind our Picture Books* was published by Fig Tree in 2019. Her novels for adults, *Delphi* (2022) and *The Modern Fairies* (2024), have been published by Fig Tree in the UK and by Avid Reader in the US. Her book for children, *The Untameables*, illustrated by Reena Makwana, was published by The Emma Press in 2024. She won the Tadeusz Bradecki Prize in 2025 for *The Modern Fairies*, an award given to works that combine story-telling fiction and non-fiction in original ways, encompassing a range of artistic genres, disciplines, cultures and subjects.

Clare Pollard was Editor of *Modern Poetry in Translation* from 2017 to 2022. She was appointed Artistic Director of the Winchester Poetry Festival in 2022. Her poem 'Pollen' – first published in *Bad Lilies* – was shortlisted for the Forward Prize for Best Single Poem 2022. She has been made an Honorary Doctor of Letters and a Fellow of the Royal Society of Literature.

CLARE POLLARD

LIVES
OF THE
FEMALE
POETS

BLOODAXE BOOKS

Copyright © Clare Pollard 2025

ISBN: 978 1 78037 747 6

First published 2025 by
Bloodaxe Books Ltd,
Eastburn,
South Park,
Hexham,
Northumberland NE46 1BS.

www.bloodaxebooks.com
For further information about Bloodaxe titles
please visit our website and join our mailing list
or write to the above address for a catalogue.

LEGAL NOTICE

All rights reserved. No part of this book may be
reproduced, stored in a retrieval system, or
transmitted in any form, or by any means, electronic,
mechanical, photocopying, recording or otherwise,
without prior written permission from Bloodaxe Books Ltd.

Requests to publish work from this book
must be sent to Bloodaxe Books Ltd.

Clare Pollard has asserted her right under
Section 77 of the Copyright, Designs and Patents Act 1988
to be identified as the author of this work.

Cover design: Neil Astley & Pamela Robertson-Pearce.

Printed in Great Britain by Bell & Bain Limited, 303 Burnfield Road,
Thornliebank, Glasgow G46 7UQ, Scotland, on acid-free paper
sourced from mills with FSC chain of custody certification.

For Rose

CONTENTS

11	Poetess
12	Inana *after Enheduanna*
14	On Emily Brontë, Aged Six
17	Pollen
18	The Head-louse
20	Praxilla
22	In Nunhead Cemetery *(for Charlotte Mew)*
23	The White Lady
26	Rye Lane
28	Sestina for Elizabeth Bishop
30	Pothos
32	Housecat
33	Cocktail List
33	*Red Witch*
34	*Margarita*
35	*French 75*
36	*Negroni*
37	*Old-Fashioned*
38	*Blue Hawaii*
39	Spoils
40	Two Sonnets for Anne Locke
42	The Sex Life of Emily Brontë
45	The Craving
46	The Pub Crawl
48	Three-Martini Afternoon
50	Improvisatrice
53	Emily Brontë and the Critic
55	Pornhub
56	Why I Won't Listen to Sad Pop Songs Any More
58	Last Word *a glosa for Wanda Coleman*
60	Poetry *after Marianne Moore*
62	The Lives of the Female Poets
71	ACKNOWLEDGEMENTS

Who shall measure the heat and violence of a poet's heart when caught and tangled in a woman's body?

VIRGINIA WOOLF

Poetess
n. dated

I have fallen once more to brooding upon my saintly Poetess.
'Poetess' has come to be a derogatory term,
an implicitly pejorative noun like 'Murderess'
in its suggestion of tepid and insipid achievement,
or else it conjures that poetess whose suicide
was misinterpreted as romantic by the college-girl mentality,
but She is the paradigmatic example of the domestic poetess,
pairing her dreamy, aphoristic poems with doodles of flowers
on her Instagram page.
My Poetess is awfully nice.
One might perceive it to be a label of contempt and condescension
that exemplifies 'the gush of the feminine'
but it is only that She commits the sin of engaging with a demographic
whose taste is often seen as a byword for bad quality,
and also She makes money.
Indeed, Aphra Behn all but equates the term with 'prostitute'.
British Poetesses make but a poor figure
in *Poems by Eminent Ladies* or *Specimens of British Poetesses*,
and it's true that the adjectives 'feminine' and 'Poetess',
when modifying poetry,
can be exchanged either with 'minor', 'popular', or 'sentimental'
without injury to sense.
Still, my Poetess presides at the female empire of the tea-table,
where She sweetens the tea
with sugar's tender hiss.

Inana

after Enheduanna

Yes, I'm unparalleled.
Robed in terrifying radiance,
I roar with the roaring storm,
my teeth crush stone,
I devour corpses
like the dog that I am.
But also, I'm deep-hearted.
Plough my vulva.
Arousal and wealth
are in my gift.
Can I offer you the milk of death?
The thing about the mountain
is it showed me no respect.
It should have rubbed its lips
in dust for me, but no.
So now I'm playing this game:
setting fire to the forests.
I'm locusts.
I'm a snake in a crevice,
a leopard on a hill,
a falcon preying on the gods.
Go on, fly away, little flappy bat!
Can you fathom me?
Of course not.
Don't you fucking dare.
Birds of sorrow
build nests in your hair.
I spread exhaustion.
This anger is too great to soothe.
I'm pushing on the lapis lazuli gate,

raising a flood of silt.
I'm speeding carnage.
I've poured blood in the rivers and
you'll drink it.
Oh dear
has your honeyed mouth filled with scum?

On Emily Brontë, Aged Six

When Emily is six she is sent to the Clergy Daughter's School. You'll recognise it as the model for Lowood school in Charlotte Brontë's Jane Eyre. Emily's three elder sisters are already there, so she's excited to be getting her own little brown pinafore and plaid cloak. The eldest, Maria and Elizabeth, have always let Emily be their kitten, who hisses when she's angry, or their puppy who crawls on their laps for a cuddle and sticks out a panting tongue. She's looking forward to their faces when they see her. But when Emily gets there slowly, like snow getting into her shoes and melting, a seeping chill enters her body: the realisation that this is not home. The realisation that this place is evil.

There is a violent pressure in the air. The whirr of birch-twig whippings. All the children are dressed in thin clothes and no boots; stomachs clamping on burnt brackish, porridge that is still somehow cold. 'SILENCE,' a teacher shouts at a cough, as clouds of breath puff and pour over books. All teachers share the same mean face. A classmate stands with a placard round her neck that reads SLATTERN. When they inspect Emily's class, moving down the line, she already knows her ridged nails will never be clean enough; her hair will always be too frizzy to stay neat. Punishment will be perpetually impending, her small body always braced for a lash.

But then: if she can't avoid punishment why bother trying? An older girl tries to stroke her hair and she hisses. She gets in trouble for biting. Teachers start to call her trouble. Perhaps it's easier if she is; if she just accepts what she is.

A typhoid epidemic sweeps the school soon afterwards – a new form of punishment, except Emily doesn't understand at first, she's too little. Maria touches her forehead, under the cap, and says 'have you got it pet?' But Emily just giggles.

'I aint got nowt! That tickles.'

Then, though, the girls begin to disappear. Just one or two at first, normal in winter with them all so malnourished. Only each day another chair is empty. Like they're being erased. The teachers don't even seem to notice. They don't mention the missing girls' names, just carry on. At dinner there's so much extra food, extra oatcake, which the remaining girls eat greedily but then you can feel the shame sluice through them like their silence has been bought. 'Where's Peggy?' Emily whispers to Elizabeth. 'Where's Esther?'

'No speaking at the table,' the teacher spits.

Deaths are announced on Sundays. 'Your schoolfellow X has died,' is the formula. 'Her teachers said that at the end she expressed a great desire to join Christ.' Liars, Emily thinks, LIARS! LIARS! As if X wanted to leave her sisters, to never hug them again!

And then Maria and Elizabeth fall ill. In reality, Maria was sent home, where she died. Elizabeth died shortly after. But in my version of the story there's a scene at the school, where Maria and Elizabeth are both ill at the same time. Stories are more compressed than real life. And, like Jane Eyre trying to see Helen Burns, Em pulls her frock over her nightdress and creeps to the infirmary.

It is full of dying little girls. Dozens of coughing, fitting, dying girls, lined up in the long room like rag-dolls in pretend beds. Feverish girls with internal bleeding and perforated bowels, caused by the contaminated water. Breathless lasses spooned lies: that

Jesus wants them back; that their maker loves them so much, he'll unmake them. Remember to say thank you! To destroy, that's a strong verb. To annihilate.

Emily Brontë was good with verbs: writhe, drag, crash, grind, struggle, yield, recoil, outstrip, tear, drive asunder. These are some of God's verbs, some of the things God does to bodies as part of His Plan.

But I'm getting ahead. Em can't crawl into a bed and embrace her sisters, though she wants to. Her whole little animal, whelp body wants to curl around and clutch them – to mew like she used to, their little kit, warming their laps. But instead she has to make do with the window. Perhaps she can get their attention. She creeps out onto the crunch of frozen pebbles, moonlit. A far away owl. She goes to the infirmary window, clings to the ledge, presses her little face to where the curtains are only half closed and she can see her sisters.

It almost looks like heaven: a heaven she is excluded from. To be cosy, together, half-asleep, books piled by their beds; the soft little tapers of the candles. But their skin is too pale. Maria's lips shine too redly, wet by a little blood.

And Em begins to knocks and knock, like a little branch might, or a ghost, and then scratch at the pane – *please please, mew mew, let me in*. But they are unconscious or don't hear her, like they are ghosts already, or she's a ghost already. And if death is what separates us from those we love like a piece of cold glass, in a way they are all already dead.

Pollen

The medium death chose, this time, was love.
Kindness, or what we'd thought was kindness, was now harm
and it was best if we just locked ourselves away,
and didn't show we cared,
and hardly lived in weeks, which were our work.
One week, though, I recall, the pollen came,
piled in our street like snow, or no, like baby hair –
I saw a boy that stroked its fur,
how, on their walk, girls kicked at it,
its carriage on the air from home to home,
over fences, yards, the apple blossom,
in through kitchen windows
to where we stared at screens on makeshift desks;
its waver on warm currents of my breath,
how my eyes streamed with tears.
Tell me that you noticed.
And did you close the window too,
uncertain, now, what you were meant to do
with all that tenderness?

The Head-louse

> 'May this tusk root out the lice of the hair and the beard'
>
> – the oldest known sentence in the earliest alphabet,
> found inscribed on a 4000-year-old ivory comb

Mark this nit. The gritty little shit.
Who can respect a faint speck?
Don't they know they're not wanted?
Irritating as fuck,
ash-flecks burning for juice.

Who can we hate if not them?
I inculcate the killer instinct.
Think of how they pierce defences,
make of friendly gestures
a smuggler's route, pervert our hospitality.

In dark, lice tap my daughter's head –
tiny unsettling thoughts.
They scratch to be let in, faceless succubi.
I scarify my children's skulls
their golden shores of hair, dredge

up dust bunnies, scaly bodies
small as not at all.
Obligate parasite. Are we obliged to host?
Host what: dirt? Motes of bloodthirst?
Their leap of faith is not my leap.

An infestation tests compassion.
A Buddhist might escort each louse
to a steep-sided bowl,

transpose those sentient seeds, but where?
Loose them where, except in hair?

O jiggling crumbs I crush then flick.
So what, wouldn't a mother chimp?
I'm only grooming fondly –
no tsunami, not a monster
before whom crowds scatter!

Your perspective's out of kilter,
they're too minuscule to matter.
Comb through damp hair, crown to tips.
It smells of sulphurous pits but the Solution
leaves things manageable; clean.

A fifteen-minute wait. Nymphs suffocate,
and now it's late. What brushes me at midnight,
finely as a web? What trembles there?
If I'm a giantess they're Jack.
The grit outwits me still: relentless irritant.

What ominous thing ticks in my hair?
A jumping pulse; the haunted house
is me, and it's the speckled ghost.
All winter, I will claw at us
then call it care. From where I am, it is.

Praxilla

> The loveliest sight I've left behind is the sun's light
> or clear stars on a dark dark sky, a full-faced moon;
> and fruits in summer – ripe cucumbers, apples, pears...
>
> PRAXILLA, 'Adonis in Hades', tr. Josephine Balmer

how drinking songs pour as wine,
    easy from your fingerbones,
how you wake to a bruise's anemone
    on your thigh or ribs,
petals round a dark stigma,
    the sour rain on the roof
of your mouth, each crushed grape
    one less eye looking,

how you please men, but still fear
    footsteps on the walk home,
how, like Adonis under Apollo,
    you're churned-up soil,
how you die in Aphrodite's arms,
    their grip too strong for mortals,
how she digs out a scream like a rose,
    her eyes blown red roses,

how, each midsummer, girls plant fennel
    in pots on flat roofs –
its rapid, leggy constellations –
    how it sprouts then withers,
so they can tear at their clothes,
    can drag up in mourning,
how you watch, far above them,
    this thing called 'catharsis',

fennel grown up too fast
        into a hot sky
where men's breath stinks of sunlight,
        and feel like Adonis,
body plundered, too touched,
        guts full of dark earth,
how you wake stiff as ground, surprised
        by your body's length in it,

then perform at their parties, polite,
        though you've teats and holes
covered up by the weeds of your clothes,
        how you know it's a test
to sink wine like a lake in the dark,
        sing the dying boy's song,
how you know what he'll miss the most –
        sunlight on drenched blades,

then bone-coloured meat of the apple,
        the pear's soft ass,
a cucumber, veined and clean-scented,
        dapple green, fever-cool,
and inside a moon lactating
        small teeth of pure light
that the bowels of men will digest
        though they have not, yet

In Nunhead Cemetery
(for Charlotte Mew)

Wings beat in tall, bare trees; a shudder.
Then your words. I remember

a bright or dark angel? Who can know?
It left no mark upon the snow.

As you stood here in the swirling, ghostly silence,
did you long for such erasure?

How raw tears can be.
What vainglorious tombs, our words.

Each snowflake's so precisely and cruelly itself:
oh they fall like all the seconds of our lives.

The White Lady

First, say this out loud:
White Lady please don't fright,
White Lady be asleep tonight.

I used to go to the mirror
hoping to see her
waiting for her soldier.
Sweet perfume of rotten roses.
She carried a taper.

You try now:
light a candle by the mirror.
Her name is scratched on walls.
Read it out three times,
touch your fingers to the planchette.
The table shudders.
Your breath is pale.

Traditionally, she appears before the death of a family member.
Traditionally, the smell of milk.
Traditionally, tears.

On your pillow,
a pearl from her snapped necklace.
It's a sleeping gown;
it's a wedding dress.

They say she takes a boat to see her lover & drowns;
hangs for murdering her husband;
starves to death in a sealed room.
They say she walks to her execution

down these stairs.
Or no, she dies in childbirth.
Or her child falls to its death
so she leaps after.
The house was built on sugar.
Can you hear cries?
If the cradle rocks you're cursed.

The table tips towards YES.
What hisses through radio static?
The baby-doll gurgles.
The planchette spells *come back*.
A boy hears her sob behind a tree.
The White Lady runs across the motorway.
After the crash,
see her melt into the wall,
a pillar of smoke…

The Lady always cradles an infant in her arms.
Is it dead?
They're both dead.
The bones of a child were discovered in the chimney
like dirty little secrets.

They say her lover fought in the War of the Roses
so she waited for him at the woods' edge
cradling her baby.
They raped her & snatched the baby.

On Christmas Eve chant:
'White Lady I've stolen your baby'
three times & she'll appear to take your child
except you have no child.
The child is always gone.

If you're reading this I'm probably dead.
If you read this three times
I'll scratch out your eyes.
I only ever want my baby,
have mercy.
Oh come back, come back.

Rye Lane

Hair which bring out the individual
I always read first, turning onto
this high street I've walked so many times –
which some weeks
was the highlight of my week,
my eeked-out pittance –
past the puddles where pigeons ruffle
feathers to uneven rooftiles;
decommissioned shopping trolleys
leashed to shops with scraps of string.
Pink nets hang on hooks
as if lamb carcasses.
Sumac, Puff Puff, Reeboks,
wet boxes stacked like ruins.
Get your rolls of vinyl
patterned with photos of salad
or like floors in Roman villas;
whiskered hellmouths of smoked catfish;
negronis; Paw Patrol balloons;
diamante swans.
There's a record shop called *Peckham Soul*.
Still a face-mask, here and there,
a tarnished 2 METRES sticker on the floor.
Still that window full of sawn-off
ladies' heads and shoulders,
left as if by their magicians –
wigs slipping above red smiles.
Seasonal lattes in the Costa,
school uniforms and onesies,
plastic bowls that translate okra
or mangos to pound coins.

In the bakery with sour-blue livery
I've bought the latticed slices
that bask beneath heat-lamps;
iced buns that sit like death-masks
in their fluted ruffs;
I've passed CASHINO by the chapel
thinking: *Dust to dust,*
purchases to ashes.
Sometimes riches
from each corner of the world
can feel so meagre.
Who is stitching? Who's not eating?
In the supermarket, paper bags
are priced-up by the entrance
ready for the foodbank trolley:
tinned soup, sanitary towels.
What waits in the dim corridors
of struggling shopping centres?
Vapes and sim cards.
Cracked sepia marble tiles
dry by increments beneath
the yellow warning-bollards.
Still, LED rainbows
flash in cheerful nail-bar windows.
Outside the Wetherspoons
a man in tracksuit and a neck-brace
smokes a cigarette.
I hope that drag's exactly what he needs.
I hope it makes his soul
tug lightly up.

Sestina for Elizabeth Bishop

It took ten years for you to find the right word,
or that's what I tell my class – your poem pinned
all that time on your wall. Or was it glued? Twelve years?
And what are years? I'm at a loss.
I'm jealous of your gold-bibbed toucan, of that drink
that's in your hand, your poems, the awards you held.

Brazil, a steep green valley, dinners held.
We're at dinner when it comes to you, that word –
we celebrate by getting drunk.
Perhaps you might recite for me, finally unpin
the poem from the wall. You've found what's lost.
We drink to drown the sound of whooshing years.

What if I haven't got ten years?
Though you've not any now. You held
the toucan's rigid body (accidentally poisoned), lost
control, blacked-out... *Inscrutable*. Was that the word?
The one you waited, so to pin?
What allows us to display such control as being drunk?

Yet the abject vulnerability of being drunk
is also perhaps what we've sought for all these years.
This work of making angels dance on heads of pins!
Perhaps we think we might be held
to account this time; by Time. *Amenable*. That word:
you waited how long? Or did you lose

all sense of time, the way we lose
our sense of it in love, or drunk:
these longing, clashing sloshing words!
I'd bang my head against your head. So many years
and how little I've been held.
No, not quite true. The hope I pin

on air is all my fault. Your mother's where I pin
the blame for your accrual of loss.
Yet hummingbirds and shooting stars! Quick, hold
your breath for the black wave! Don't drink
the wave, Elizabeth! A toast to better years!
I want to call you darling, kiss out words

I've held so precious, get word-drunk
to have you pin down, so precisely, every loss.
How many years must I wait for a word?

Pothos

Alexander in Egypt,
in his buffetted tent,
reads his much-loved copy of *The Iliad*,
the one he keeps beneath his pillow,
as dark tugs pegs,
sand pressed in prints on the rug,
his tongue mint-flavoured from tea,
rough-tongued camels gargling thickly,
as my son, in his school hall,
in assembly,
in Adidas grey marl pants,
long-sleeved T-shirt,
sheet loosely pinned for a toga,
bearing the cardboard sign –
ALEXANDER THE GREAT –
his long curls still notionally blond, beautiful
in that way boys are at their beginning,
voice unbroken,
throws his throat back, almost arrogant, sings:
I wanted more, more, more,
and we whoop as Alexander thinks of Persia,
gold and alabaster,
the governor dragged to death from a cart in Gaza
because it reminded him of the passage about Hector,
though it felt strangely unpoetic in the doing,
as if no Gods were watching,
and my son wants to see the world
as do the children of Gaza,
who my son and I speak little of
though that violence is an ambience,
but Alexander wants to talk, he's lonely

and wonders aloud to Ptolemy
if the world might not be big enough,
that he might run out of territory,
though he surely knows the borders
that will stop him are temporal
and not spatial,
that he won't reach the world's edge,
spoken of by Aristotle,
beyond the Hindu Kush
where white mist spills into abyss,
but a mosquito's tiny vengeance
will open an inferno,
a feverish ledge to end
his petty empire of days
at thirty-two – total defeat –
and I know I mustn't pity him
but we can't pity everyone
and he's my son.

Housecat

I hate myself, I think.

I wouldn't say that aloud though,
even to myself, alone.
I'm silent on my own, but for the clink
of dishes, the wet sound
of coffee's wash against my teeth.

Our neighbours' cat,
voluptuous with canned meat,
stares at me from its spill of sun.
That vacant splat of face!
The way they groom themselves disgusts me,
the small pink tongue of self-regard.

Even when I say I hate myself
inside my skull
I flinch a bit,
it's so attention seeking.
I don't know whose.

COCKTAIL LIST

Red Witch

Lager, cider, Pernod and black
and a cheap pint of frog's blood
is conjured.
Bodies swell in this thumping cellar,
the auspicious dark.
Whose drink?
It's mine. I'm fifteen
in my Wonderbra,
slogan tee that spells *Pussy Galore.*
For my next drink he'll buy something harder:
Slippery Nipple perhaps or a Blowjob.
'…I SAID TWO ORGASMS PLEASE…'
Tacky fingers alight
on the red of an Amsterdam window.
I swallow it, curse or pact.

Margarita

To try my first we crossed the border to Tijuana.
I was with two other girls.
Margarita is a girl's name.
It was two-for-one, so we lined the drinks up on the bar.
I'm obviously not proud of myself.
The faded, perforated banners were absolutely still.
It was hot and everything was very parched –
rimmed with glare
and salty-edged.
My lips were salt flats.
Margarita-mix the colour of standing water
or sun seen through an arid haze.
I could taste the agave, that spiky succulent
pollinated by hummingbirds and greater long-nosed bats,
whose yellow flowers produce several thousand mostly sterile seeds
before they die.
A Zonkey was caked in dry paint.
A man opened his shirt and flashed his dusty erection at us,
the driest thing we'd ever seen.

French 75

Glamour!
The word itself is an enchantment.
What could be more glamorous
than Harry's New York Bar in 1920s Paris?
Fuck yes Paris.
You do know Ernest Hemingway and Rita Hayworth drank there?
That James Bond *lost his virginity* after visiting Harry's Bar?
I'm wearing heels.
I'm out out and it's a cold clear night of stars.
You need lemon juice and sugar-syrup but the main thing is
there is *gin* in your *Champagne*.
Is it like being shelled by a French 75mm field gun?
Isn't for me to say,
but it feels risky
in the right way,
as the sparkles form tiny spiral stairways
that I tensely ascend.

Negroni

After my child was born it was the first drink I wanted.
I had the three bottles lined up in my kitchen
near the baby's bottle, steriliser and teats.
Adulthood in a glass; a bitter release,
like the relief you imagine death to be except
if you're dead, of course, you can't feel relief.
It was something for me,
when I had my breath back for my own.
Equal parts gin, Italian vermouth,
and Campari the colour of insects
crushed under your nails,
of a birthing pool.
Sometimes I feel my eyes in my sockets,
the blood slip through its slim tubes,
the heart clench, unasked.
I heard the baby breathe in a basket,
in little white things
as I let that red strobe through me –
an *aperitivo* to whet my nerve.

Old-Fashioned

Every time I try to stir one
there's an inner voice that whispers:
orange peel is not a mixer,
sugarcubes are not a mixer.

Blue Hawaii

It's hard to say anyone deserves one,
yet here it is:
the blue of a chlorinated hot-tub,
scented like suntan lotion.
The Blue Hawaii was created in 1957 by Harry Yee,
head bartender of the Hilton Hawaiian Village
and is named for the Elvis song.
Blue Curaçao is named for the Caribbean island
colonised by the Dutch;
is flavoured by the peel
of the bitter and inedible laraha fruit.
Cream of Sky.
It slips down a bit too easily
as I gnaw a cherry off a cocktail umbrella
invented during the Great Depression
as a form of escapism.
I'm going to have to forgive myself.

Spoils

> I hold my honey and I store my bread
> In little jars and cabinets of my will
>
> GWENDOLYN BROOKS

Honey's always seemed too sweet.
A mawkish gold I never earned.
The labouring colony;
the twelve lost lives;
the hundred blooms –
primrose, foxglove, poppy – inching
lightward from cracked seed
to open themselves up
for what?
One spoonful, gulped.

Happiness, too,
is something I can hardly bear to taste.
I take a photograph instead:
my daughter at the golden hour,
as she huffs out the golden flames
that cower
on cloying shop-bought cake
that she's done nothing to deserve
except be born.

My poems line up on the shelves!
All the little jars
of joy that I have hoarded from this world
for whom? For when?
The date encroaches
when they'll spoil.

They're spoiling now.

Two Sonnets for Anne Locke

    I

'A sonnet is a moment's monument,'
so Dante Gabriel Rossetti said,
and Shakespeare knew a rose's short-lived scent
could be distilled in verse to never fade,
whilst Wyatt's lust was to a lustre wrought
within fourteen immortal, pulsing lines –
eight lines, and then the turn – a change of thought.
These tiny mausoleums for the mind!

But men sit on the canon's pedestals
and they have made no monument for you
although, in English, you were first to scrawl
a sonnet sequence to enshrine your truth.

Your pain's perfect pentameter, Anne Locke,
is our inheritance if we would look.

II

John Donne begged God to batter at his heart –
for God to break, blow, burn him to the ground
within each little song, as though his art
might phoenix him; might cauterise his wound.
Hopkins was heartburn; gall. He groped, like you,
for grace, his sweating self in night's black bed,
knowing that's god's surveillance sees the truth.
There's no safe place to hide the things you did.

The sonnet's always driven by desire,
a thing some claim that women don't possess –
but something drove you, Anne, into that fire
to grasp each burning rhyme, each searing stress,

to stuff your torment in each sonnet's box.
I touch the ash – still warm – and am unlocked.

On the Sex Life of Emily Brontë

It seems unlikely that Emily Brontë ever had a lover or even an object for her romantic feelings. There have been attempts to link her to her father's handsome assistant curate, William Weightman – who charmed all the sisters before he died suddenly of cholera – but from the evidence we have, including Anne's novel *Agnes Grey*, it is likely that his strongest bond was with Anne, the conventionally prettier, more pious sister.

This absence has driven biographers slightly mad. One constructed a theory that Emily bore or aborted a child during her six-month stay in Halifax, but there is no evidence to support it. In 1936 another biographer, Virginia Moore, wrote the astonishingly titled 'The Life and Eager Death of Emily Brontë' in which she announced to the world – after discerning a faint name pencilled next to a poem in one of her manuscripts – that she had discovered Emily's secret love. The name was, drumroll… Louis Parensell! Except it wasn't true. The pencil marks actually read 'Love's Farewell', an alternative poem title. It seems that Emily died a virgin.

The genius of *Wuthering Heights* is that this very immature, adolescent fantasy about love isn't based on any experience or reality at all, and that's also what makes it sort of evil. It's a depiction of love by someone who knows nothing about it, full of definitions of love that are simply wrong ('He's more myself than I am.' Who feels that? Whoever felt that?). It depicts romantic love at an intensity that is impossible. But she makes it feel so real, so convincing, that we want to believe. Some small part of us does believe. We want the thunderstorms and lightning, then spend our whole lives looking for a love like that and we never find it. We are tragically misled.

I don't think she had a lover but I think she masturbated. That sounds awful, doesn't it? I mean, it sounds so intrusive, when she was an actual person who was alive once – a real, sentient, private person. What right do I have, to intrude into her thoughts and sniff her bedding? A bit of me thinks it's fine, because it's 200 years ago, but what does it matter if its 200 years or one? She's still a real person, not my doll.

But art is art. This scene feels necessary. Because she's so full of passion, so embodied. Think about that bit in *Wuthering Heights*: 'Heaven did not seem to be my home and I broke my heart with weeping to come back to earth; and the angels were so angry that they flung me out into the middle of the heath on the top of Wuthering Heights; where I woke sobbing for joy.'

I don't think she'd have been worried about maintaining her purity for her future husband or anything. She would have watched the animals rubbing against each other and felt curious; wondered what relief they felt. And the whole Gondal world she and Anne created is so adolescent-sexual-fantasy. That poem that begins 'I am the only being whose doom / no tongue would ask no eye would mourn…' (I know, most eyes would roll), has that great line: 'In secret pleasure, secret tears, / This changeful life has slipped away.' Emily the laureate of secret pleasure.

So at night, in her bed, at first she practises kissing – the back of her hand, the hole in her fist, the pillow. Then, she takes it further, around that time of the month – just after your period, when you get horny like a dog on heat, like you're losing your mind, and she's about fifteen too, a hormonal nightmare – in my version, she tries with the pillow between her legs, rocking against it like an animal might. And she can feel something mounting, but also a sense it's not enough – the feeling isn't sharp enough. She is so full up with longing; she needs to get to the source of the ache and excise it. A pin to get the splinter out.

So Emily uses her fingers, then. Touches the meat of herself, softly, exploring. It is hot and slick and messy, petalled like a wild rose, oh god. And the person she imagines touching her is probably an early version of Heathcliff. One of A.G.A.'s lovers in Gondal: Alexander of Elbë, Fernando De Samara, Alfred Sidonia of Aspin Castle. She's not started *Wuthering Heights* yet, but he's forming in her imagination, looking at her with such aching eyes. Want in human form.

Emily Brontë touches her lips and her clit, rubbing, rubbing, sliding, and she feels something coming – perhaps the thing she's always longed for. Or no, the opposite, some terrible event! It will destroy her! Is it too late to stop? He is kissing her in front of the fire, and his hand reaches down and Ah! Ah! Ah! *No! Help! It's too much!* It builds in her like the storm; she is puppetted; pinned and tortured; she has lost control – is begging her pillow: help me, save me...

I think of an image from a Sylvia Plath poem, 'The Rabbit-Catcher', where the trap shuts around the rabbit, squeezing it – Emily's cunt gripping down on her fingers like a trap might on some trembling animal. The spasms are so intense, so frightening, she jerks her fingers away as from an electric shock, but the aftershocks continue. Falling back, fading spasms shuddering through her as she lies astonished, like windows opening and slamming shut in a haunted house.

The Craving

A word I hear a lot now is 'resilience'.
I like to be rejected very privately,
ideally via an email or a letter I can open
in a locked bathroom.
I'm really absolutely fine.
Sometimes I think that pity's
all they want to give me.
Couldn't I let myself be held just once?
Blurt out a sob or something?
Far from here, there's an enchanted castle,
in its garden, such delectable golden fruit
that for a second mouthful
you'd bargain all you have:
home, sanity, your firstborn child.
I think it tastes of giving up,
the relief of it.
No, you can't make me.

The Pub Crawl

It starts with a weak shandy
with her father in the beer-garden,
like a glass of fitful summer sleep.
A pint of snakebite next, in that bar with soft-porn on the screens –
it tickles as the boy who bought it yells into her ear –
then the fresher's pint, tequila slammer chaser
(how grotesque, to lick the toad of her clenched hand).
Remember Stella Artois?
They drink one because it's very expensive, then they stop.
A crisp, small beer served with jamon and a *gilda* –
olive, anchovy and pickled chilli on a skewer –
in Bilbāo, in early evening's busy glamour.
Perhaps this is the best beer?
Such pleasure to be truly quenched.
One round at The Golden Heart, under a Tracy Emin neon.
The Shakespeare, The Prince George, The Marquis, The Pride.
A darts board; Turkish carpet; Scampi Fries.
A zero-alcohol beer she pretends is real,
syrupy like the word nursery,
then a cheeky pint with him in the afternoon,
in a pub with those little wooden windows,
a snug by a fire,
the baby napping in the pram.
The pint she drinks alone on a Friday night
because she's got to go home and do bedtime
and it's Friday damn it,
whilst handsome young princes rescue glass turrets.
The can of 'Pump up the Jam'
where she realises she's middle aged
because it actually calls itself a 'Jam Doughnut Pale Ale'.

The pint that makes her need a piss
in freezing toilets with a flooded floor and crude scraped graffiti
like the toilets when she was sixteen,
so she sits on the toilet trying to concentrate, telling herself:
you're alive now! Remember this!
For fuck's sake!
REMEMBER YOU'RE ALIVE!
The last pint sits, redolent, on its damp mat.
She's old now, eating pig-skin with musty fingers
whilst the bell rings for kicking out.
They are putting up the chairs.

Three-Martini Afternoon

The first in a glass
like a tornado
brought to heel.

How the olive
with its red heart
makes a Dead Sea.

Children can be trained
to mix martinis
to deliver to your study

if you wish.
I eat the free potato chips.
Order another looking-glass,

sip its frigid rim,
my piss-hole in the snow.
It's ritzy at The Ritz

plus, basically, just vodka neat –
a blowtorch at white heat
is quite the taste!

Clear spirit
as in fugue; electroshock.
A good martini's always

haunted by vermouth's
bone-dry and colourless
monoxide.

The others?
Oh, they caught their ride,
but stir one more.

I've got this thirst this thirst.

Improvisatrice
(for L.E.L. [Letitia Elizabeth Landon], 1802-1838)

What the hell, L.E.L?
I recognise the start –
you were an 'Infant genius'
with an ambitious heart,

hair worn *à l'enfant*
above the swansdown muff.
But you lay down for your editor
to earn your puff.

Soon ten thousand pens
in inky pots leapt up!
Surely Bryon's sister?
And soon too, up puffed

your wreath of white roses,
your decolletage,
made blowsy by the joy
of a worm twice your age

who made you pass babies
as if through a mirror
to win the golden violet
at the literary dinner,

or position of songbird
in *The Gazette*'s cage;
a nightingale's stained mouth;
a page, the age, the rage.

You burnt both candle ends,
kept up the rustling show,
contributing the favours,
his Echo, his echo.

Did Keats say Truth is beauty?
A romantic idea!
But none *dares to say*
What none will choose to hear.

You were a plucky plucker
of the lyre's eternal Lies,
even as the print-run plunged.
No 'tears' without a fire,

in this masque called literature
you hid thoughts in plain view,
wept for fallen women
then fucked for a review.

Vile link in earth's weary chain
sustained by sips of fame –
but Flattery's a golden sieve
that left the scum of shame.

You faked it beyond fake,
faked it with the truth
and girls must never say so,
but, sure, I fake it too.

(My inner thoughts are wrong ones
like everybody's
and were I to confess them
the right would cancel me).

LOL, L.E.L.
They tarnished your name.
Your ladylike white riddles
were suddenly fair game –

E.B.B. and Rossetti
perhaps could hear your truth.
Are you *Aurora Leigh*?
Did you gobble goblin fruit?

But Woolf's *Orlando* found
your words insipid puke –
knocked ink to mask your lyrics,
its darkness blotting you.

And now you are forgotten
except your rumoured murder
in Cape Coast Castle, Ghana.
(Such post-Bryonic drama!)

They found you by your desk.
You were only thirty-six.
The ocean churning lines;
Prussic acid on your lips.

Did you do it for the hell?
Did you do it to be real?
Suicidal ideation?
Or only for the feels?

And did the red and white ants
eat away your face?
In my mind's eye: cannons
circumscribe the place.

On Emily Brontë and the Critic

There were several anonymous reviewers who laid into *Wuthering Heights*, but I imagine one character – I make a compound character. Youngish, perhaps 30, still hungry, keen to be a provocateur. But also broke: bar bills; the price of laudanum, that easeful tincture with which he self-medicates. Mussed hair, tall for his time, stooping to enter doorways, always an edge of slur to his voice. A squib of rum to take the edge off his kids screaming in the next room; to help him think of someone else when he fucks his wife, who is ruined down there from four children already.

Once I heard a man say that watching his wife give birth was like watching someone burn down his favourite pub. I imagine the reviewer has that energy.

Anon. Anon who smells blood when *Wuthering Heights* lands on his desk. Because it's so – so uncivilised, so coarse. And better yet he can smell that it's by a woman. Lockwood doesn't fool him, the frame – this is a book in a female domestic's voice. A book about love. It's pulsing with female desire, the desire to possess men utterly, to yoke them to the meat and gristle of existence, to drag them into their graves. It revolts him. What happened to craft? What happened to learning? Oh the boys are going to love this one! He licks his lips a little as he dips his pen in the ink. His little whip.

He loves the pursuit. This is the same Anon who has called Mary Shelley's novels 'sickening, diseased and full of stupid cruelties'. Who will label Anne Brontë's second novel *The Tenant of Wildfell Hall* 'unreadable' in its 'disgustingly truthful minuteness' and add that 'Unless our authoress can contrive to refine and elevate her general notions of all human and divine things, we shall be glad to learn that she is not intending to add another work to those which have already been produced by her pen.' He will also soon enjoy writing that Elizabeth Gaskell is 'all woman' and 'makes a creditable effort to overcome her natural deficiencies but all in vain, as women necessarily know little about the cotton industry and have no right to add to the confusion by writing about it'. Now though, it is Emily's turn to be punished.

'This book is so rude', the reviewer begins, 'So unfinished, baffling, brutal and careless, that we are perplexed to announce an opinion on it, or to hazard a conjecture on the future career of the author. Read *Jane Eyre* is our advice, but burn *Wuthering Heights*. There is an old saying that those who eat toasted cheese at night will dream of Lucifer. The author of *Wuthering Heights* has evidently eaten toasted cheese, and nightmares, through which devils and wolves howl, make bad novels. How a human being could have attempted such a book as the present without committing suicide before he had finished a dozen chapters, is a mystery. This reader was shocked, disgusted and sickened by the diabolical hate and vengeance. Ellis Bell is a spendthrift of malice, profanity, depravity and unnatural horrors.'

When Emily reads this, in a private corner behind a locked door, she stifles a cry; feels her legs falter. Dying of thirst, she has longed so much for a clear deep draught from this oasis, but now her lips close on sand. No no no no.

Self-belief can only take you so far. In the hope she might somehow be recognised she has taken risks, terrible risks, and sees now she has failed. Instead, she is only to be recognised as a slut might be recognised – shamed and mocked by this man because he recognises he is Somebody and she is Nobody; her reputation soiled and shat on. She has exposed herself. She has made poppets of herself, and had them sent out far and wide to people who own pins.

Pornhub

You know I know you watch it – subcutaneous fat; the jiggling ducts; engorgement; glans; mons Venus; blood hood; cauldron; little bridle loosed as some slut stepmom's juice explodes, apparently: with a single drip, off-white, like candlewax, and moaning like she might if it was staged to blackmail your father. Penis from the Latin, meaning tail. Afterwards, you close the window, sad as god – or as god's dog who waits at god's shut door; who'd hoped the shudder meant that god was home. Why stepmoms, little Oedipus? Riddle me that, next time you're bored. Bad stepsister gets POUNDING. You wag for meat; for something plucked – a grandmother or rose, at best, infested by some worm that eats a hole; Snow White's liver; glassy slipper; anal massage; mirror mirror. Sex is so interior. But you're outside, and they are too: you watch them pose themselves for you and act their arses off, but still it ends the same: creampie! The afterwards as spoilt before; as spluttered spit; as *blind my eyes*. Cinders. Slapstick. What if I told you that I've watched you watch them? Send money to my bank account.

Why I Can't Listen to Sad Pop Songs Any More

Rain pours down like catharsis.
She listens to Shawn Mendes,
bedroom door shut, floor a litter

of Kens, lipbalms and post-its,
striking tragic little poses
in the mirror as she mouths

or emotes, the kids now say,
fingers making feathered hearts,
whilst he sings of needing kisses

where it hurts, of needing stitches,
whilst I'm hanging up the laundry
in the spare room, on the dryer –

every day it needs redoing –
hanging black sails of a dark wash
and I feel like going under.

In *The Odyssey*, the crew
watch the rain speckle the deck,
but the sirens' powerballads

about wanting something back
are muted by the wax,
whilst, lashed to the mast,

only Odysseus can hear them
cheep the song 'Selfpity'
that goes *shoo-be-doo... poor me...*

heart-break-ache-make-me-good.
Lalala, I will not listen.
I can't have again or more,

such music's an enchantment
sung to stop me getting home,
when I am here.

Last Word

a glosa for Wanda Coleman

> May you be kept out of the heaven
> From which you have kept others
> May no one hear your last words
> May a small rodent eat your last words
>
> WANDA COLEMAN, 'Black-Handed Curse'

I drank my first *Last Word* at a fortieth.
Green Chartreuse is an inscrutable
elixir for long life
distilled by Carthusian monks
to taste like Ophelia's speech in Act IV.
A cocktail list says *Carpe Diem*.
I wish I could have raised a glass to you, Wanda,
but you are dead, and whilst alive
were often stupidly forgotten.
Which cunts kept you from the heaven

of earthly recognition?
Xanadu shut its door to you.
Maraschino's wrought from flesh and pits.
I shake until it hurts.
Lime stings my cuts.
I don't know why I bother.
Perhaps I need it to cut through
the scuttlebugs and beans,
despair's stormcloud of dither
from which your words kept others

but you couldn't steal its thunder.
Did I keep you from heaven?
Some cunt like me
drank champagne at that literary party.

It's a long time since I drank champagne
Chekhov said before he died (slurred?)
I strain the cocktail in the glass.
I need help bad, man. Jimi Hendrix's
last words – or last heard.
May no one hear my last words.

A cocktail is a ritual
to make a minute immortal.
It ought to be precise and memorable.
This one's the green of kryptonite.
I fear my last word will be 'help'.
Poets are so absurd
and vulnerable.
All my courage lies unread
but Wanda, I swear your words are heard.
May a small rodent, tenderly, eat my words.

Poetry
after Marianne Moore

I, too, dislike it. What do you hope to obtain from this poem, after all?
   To be told you're a good girl? That it will be okay? It really won't.
   Perhaps you wish to admire your own feelings
     as in a mirror?
     To hear that the nasturtium's leaves
       cup their little flowers like hell-flames against high wind?

Perhaps you read out of desire for light music, cultural clout, to meditate
   with mindfulness on the golden rose's curdling.
   No, no, I've got it – a prayer – a spell to utter
     on breath or in skull,
     solicit meaning or control.
       And I, of course, want to make time stand still. Or to be

a part, to put it generously, of literature's great, long conversation.
   Or somewhere to put this excess of love, though what does it help the
                                        rain I'm moved
   by the shining quietness of its multitudes, swearing:
     I love you, as if the rain is a boy
     that I've chased to an airport?
       I am embarrassing the rain. The rain would say: 'shut up mum'.

Or, wait, I write to tell you about my recurring dream. I'm curled in a ball,
   in a hole – an animal licking itself – and can smell the earth contract,
                                               world shrink
   to soil on my skin, but the shrinking doesn't stop,
     it occurs within my edges,
     it's death, I think, though there's never quite
       relief, only the ending juddering through me as some beast through
                                                         a gate…

Have you found what you want in this poem yet? Truthfully, I hope
                              you're happy.
  It's grim, the way I'm never dead and neither are you, in this zombie
                                apocalypse
called poetry. Don't the golden buds always push back through?
   Which is to say, the flames.
   Now, put this book down, step away,
      the galaxy still on your skin like a sheet of dirt.

The Lives of the Female Poets

/
A was a lioness.
Created something that no one had created before –
high priestess of the goddess of conquest,

>   milk of death in her mouth...
>   O impetuous wild cow!

The significance of A was not recognised until Adam Falkenstein
published an article in 1958.

/
B wrote epitaphs
for those who crossed the pale stream:
dear, short-lived babes;
a pet cicada in his tiny tomb.

It is said she cured a blind man
and was called the female Homer, for a while.

/
C was well thought of into the fifth century,
mentioned alongside Plato, Cicero, Martial, and Juvenal.
Now she is naked under linen,
with Calenus inside her,
in the two surviving lines of iambic trimeter.

/
D rose up to Rank Two, or Favourite Beauty;
was accused of witchcraft
like a moon-shaped fan

that when autumn comes is put into a box.
D is remembered for her 'Song of Resentment',
though there is a certain historical doubt about the attribution of this song

/

E was a concubine who fled court. E founded the monastery of Sainte-
Croix. E ate only legumes or pale greens. Legend has it that E's fingers
healed; eeked tenderness from wolves; wrote poems (non-extant)

/

F was noted for writing in the genre of incitement to vengeance, or **taḥrīḍ**.
Scholars debate whether F's work was fabricated in the medieval period.

/

G supported her family by writing for Dauphines, Queens,
for Burgundy or Orleans.
Soul incarcerated in body,
petals caving by abbey walls…
The goldfinch sang teLLIT-teLLIT-teLLIT.

In *Querelle du Roman de la Rose*
G attacked the misogyny of Jean de Meun's *Romance of the Rose*
by belittling her own writing style in a rhetorical strategy known as antiphrasis.

/

H was an Andalusian princess.
Walked without hijab, in translucence.
Instructed women of all classes in poetry.
Fell in love with Ibn Zaydun,
who betrayed H,
then wrote numerous verses on the subject:

> for me you were nothing but a sweetmeat I bit,
> tossing away the crust to be gnawed on by a rat.

It is thanks to her role as Ibn Zaydun's muse that any of H's works
survives.

/

I married an official and had a bad marriage. I either had an affair or
committed suicide and after I died, all the poetry I had written was
burned.

/

        J as in Jasmine   refused dress   was meat, hair, scent

              was subject to hagiographic mythological claims

       this world is Shiva's eye   *what can you*   *cover and conceal?*

/

K loved her slave. One official reported that his servant had observed the
slave sleeping and eating in the room next to his mistress' bedchamber.
It was rumoured that K had mothered a daughter by her slave. The
officials now argued this was a case of public morality. Servants were
tortured to investigate the claim. K's slave died during interrogation and
more than 40 people were arrested. Some members of the government
argued death was too strong a punishment for a royal woman, but it was
agreed to be more respectful than torture, so K was forced to kill herself.

/

L was born into a family of ropemakers, surgeons and butchers;
was a knight on horseback in male dress,
la belle Amazone – angelface –
sonneteer –
think of the word *ravish*.

In 1560 Calvin referred to L cross-dressing,
calling her a *plebeia meretrix* or *common whore*.

/
M lulled her baby,
wretched with snot,
retching up milk,
nightmare hot.

Rock rock rock rock.
The child who doesn't cry will be spared by the hyenas.

/
N was put on the rack.

The wine was just wine,
the bread just bread,
a negation in N's throat.

N burnt slowly.

/
O was the first Englishwoman to assert herself as a professional poet.
O spoke to the astrologer about her miscarriages;
felt Will Shakespeare's tongue
on her mouth's tender ceiling –
fingers scrawling in that ink, her hair [

      ] O O O

/
P had nine children and wrote poems about her gout. Jonathan Swift called her one of his 'triumfeminate'. A city shower…wigs…decanted wine… How P laughed at his bon mots!

/
Q was her father's favourite daughter:
slender, two moles, pearls at the throat.

Q wrote under the pseudonym 'Hidden One';
was imprisoned by her father for 20 years in a fort.

It has been theorised the crime was being a poetess,
anathema to her father's orthodox thought.

/
R was stolen, shipped, sold;
taught to read classics by twelve;
write poems by fourteen
that promised those 'black as Cain, / May be refin'd…'

R, by thirty-one, had refin'd herself to free;
to scullery maid;
angel.

/
S was nicknamed Muffy or Pet.
'Delicious tainted butter'
wolfed down by Scott, Stevenson and Twain.
Her secret?
Dying a month short of her ninth birthday.

/
T was born outside the Pale.
Parting grass,
a taste of pear.
Fucked her girlfriends –
                        smelted –
beneath her velvet throw…

Stalin's government considered homosexuality a disease,
so her poems were declared unlawful.

/
U was from Uruguay.
Married Enrique Job Reyes in August 1913
and left him a month later.

For one blue minute, colts smoked through the fields.

After their divorce was finalised,
he shot her twice in the head.

/
V's *The Ghetto and Other Poems* was a popular success,
until she fell out of critical favour due to her impassioned, realistic verse.

/
– W won the bardic crown twice. How did she fail to win it?
– She was accused of cheating twice.

/
X lacked a rib,
so, after the divorce, was given few visiting rights.
Her son was brought up to believe his mother
had abandoned him for poetry and sex;
'to sin the sin of pleasure'.

X was ablaze – attacked –
(were they howling like that
just to earn a day's plate of basmati rice?)
The official story is that X swerved her car
to avoid an oncoming school-bus.

/
Y vanished.

/
Z reads that, historically, there are few women poets, and they do not stand comparison with the best men. Their absence from the canon is due to illiteracy or domesticity; a lack of opportunity.

The editors of the anthology point out that, had they not excluded poets under sixty, they might have found more women amongst their contemporaries (though only time will tell if any endure beyond the momentary).

Z dreams that she is A
[
    ] dreams deathless [
       ] milk

ACKNOWLEDGEMENTS

Acknowledgements are due to the editors of the following publications where some of these poems first appeared: *Bad Lilies*, *Basket*, *bath magg*, *Berlin Lit*, *Black Iris*, *Perverse*, *Poetry Birmingham Literary Journal*, *Poetry London*, *The Poetry Review* and *The Idler*.

The poem 'The Lives of the Female Poets' was first published as a short pamphlet by Bad Betty.

'Cocktail List' was published by Blown Rose as part of their Handbook series.

'The White Lady' was commissioned by Sidekick Books for their anthology *Ten Poets Tell You Their Favourite Ghost Story*.

'Two Sonnets for Anne Locke' were written for the BBC Radio 3 Sunday Feature *Unlocking Anne* – many thanks to the producer Sarah Shebbeare for involving me in the project.

'Poetess' is a largely found poem, collaged from search-engine results for the term poetess.

The Lives of The Female Poets is inspired by and in memory of: Enheduanna, Anyte of Tegea, Sulpicia, Consort Ban, Radegund, Al-Ḥujayjah, Christine de Pizan, Wallada, Zhu Shuzhen, Akka Mahadevi, Yi Guji, Louise Labé, a Kenyan mother, Anne Askew, Emilia Lanier, Mary Barber, Zeb-un-Niss, Phillis Wheatley, Marjorie Fleming, Sophia Parnok, Delmira Agustini, Lola Ridge, Eluned Phillips, Forough Farrokhzād and Rosemary Tonks. I have quoted liberally from their Wikipedia pages.

A special thankyou to Neil Astley, who has published me since my first collection over 25 years ago, and who suggested I read the brilliantly researched biography *L.E.L.: The Lost Life and Mysterious Death of the 'Female Byron'* by Lucasta Miller to whom I am greatly indebted. And to Hannah Sullivan for her careful reading of the manuscript, and suggestion of a poem beginning with Marianne Moore's line 'I, too, dislike poetry'.

EU DECLARATION OF GPSR CONFORMITY

Books published by Bloodaxe Books are identified by the EAN/ISBN printed above our address on the copyright page and manufactured by the printer whose address is noted below. This declaration of conformity is issued under the sole responsibility of the publisher, the object of declaration being each individual book produced in conformity with the relevant EU harmonisation legislation with no known hazards or warnings, and is made on behalf of Bloodaxe Books Ltd on 25 September 2025 by Neil Astley, Managing Director, editor@bloodaxebooks.com.

No part of this book may be used or reproduced in any manner for the purpose of training artificial intelligence technologies or systems. The publisher expressly reserves *Lives of the Female Poets* from the text and data mining exception in accordance with European Parliament Directive (EU) 2019/790.

MIX
Paper | Supporting responsible forestry
FSC
www.fsc.org   FSC® C007785